Fiji

A Tourist Encyclopedia

Mark M Karl

Table of content

Chapter 1
>   **Introduction to Fiji**

Chapter 2
>   **Planning Your Trip**

Chapter 3
>   **Top Destinations**

Chapter 4
>   **Exploring Fijian Culture**

Chapter 5
>   **Outdoor Adventures and Activities**

Chapter 6
>   **Practical Tips and Safety**

Chapter 7
>   **Introduction to Fijian cuisine**

Chapter 8

Sustainability and Responsible Tourism

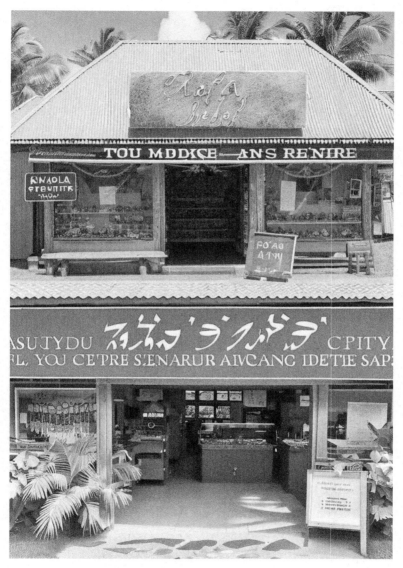

A Jewelry shop in Fiji

Chapter 1

Introduction to Fiji

Overview of Fiji's Geography: Fiji is an archipelago situated in the South Pacific Ocean, encompassing 333 islands, of which roughly 110 are inhabited. The two major islands are Viti Levu and Vanua Levu. The nation is noted for its outstanding natural beauty, with attractive beaches, coral reefs, lush jungles, and volcanic scenery. Fiji is located in the Melanesian area, northeast of New Zealand and east of Australia. Its entire land area is roughly 18,270 square kilometers (7,056 square miles).

History of Fiji: Fiji's history extends back thousands of years when the islands were initially populated by the Lapita people, thought to be predecessors of the Polynesians. European discovery of Fiji started in the 17th century, with Dutch and British navigators establishing contact. The islands came under British rule in the 19th century and remained a British colony until winning independence in 1970. Throughout its history, Fiji has endured periods of tribal wars, colonial domination, and political upheavals. Today, it is a parliamentary democracy with a rich cultural past.

Culture of Fiji: Fiji has a diversified and lively culture created by its indigenous Fijian people, as well as influences from Indian, European, and Chinese groups. The Fijian people are noted for their warm hospitality and a strong sense of community. Traditional practices, rituals, and ceremonies play a prominent part in Fijian life, including the kava ceremony, meke dances, and firewalking rites. Music, storytelling, and handicrafts are vital components of Fijian culture.

The Fijian Way of Life: The Fijian way of life focuses on the idea of "bula," which implies life, health, and happiness. Fijians have a calm and welcoming attitude, emphasizing family, community, and respect for elders. The traditional village system remains vital, with chiefs (turaga ni koro) functioning as communal leaders. Fijians participate in subsistence agriculture, fishing, and handicrafts. Rugby is a cherished sport in Fiji, sometimes referred to as the national sport, and plays a key part in the cultural fabric of the country.

Official Languages, Currency, and Time Zone: The official languages of Fiji are English, Fijian, and Hindi. English serves as the predominant language for government, business, and education, but Fijian and Hindi are widely used by the community. The Fijian language is part of the Austronesian language family, especially the Malayo-Polynesian branch. Hindi is spoken by the Indo-Fijian people, descendants of indentured workers transported from India during British colonial periods.

The currency of Fiji is the Fijian dollar (FJD). It is best to convert cash upon arrival or utilize ATMs, which are commonly accessible in metropolitan areas. Credit cards are accepted in most hotels, restaurants, and tourism enterprises.

Fiji observes Fiji Standard Time (FST), which is 12 hours ahead of Coordinated Universal Time (UTC+12). The nation does not follow daylight saving time, hence the time difference may vary based on the time zone of the visitor's home country.

These short introductions offer an overview of Fiji's geography, history, culture, the way of life of its people, as well as information on the official languages, currency, and time zone. Exploring these parts of Fiji's identity might boost one's knowledge and enjoyment of this amazing place.

Chapter 2

Planning Your Trip

Best Time to Visit Fiji and Considerations for Different Seasons:
Fiji offers a tropical environment throughout the year, making it an attractive location for vacationers seeking warm weather and gorgeous beaches. However, there are several aspects to bear in mind while arranging your visit:

High Season (May through October):

The dry season in Fiji, with reduced humidity and colder temperatures.
Ideal for outdoor activities like snorkeling, diving, and visiting the islands.
June to September is especially popular owing to school vacations in Australia and New Zealand, so anticipate higher costs and more people.
Booking rooms and flights in advance is suggested during this season.
Shoulder Season (April and November):

Transitional months with beautiful weather and fewer people compared to the hot season.

Prices for rooms and flights may be cheaper during this time.

It's an excellent time to come if you want a calmer ambiance yet still want to enjoy nice weather.

Wet Season (December to March):

Fiji's rainy season suffers greater temperatures, humidity, and frequent rains, yet it's still feasible to enjoy your vacation.

Rain showers are typically short-lived, and the weather might be unpredictable.

The rainy season brings lush greenery, bright scenery, and the chance to enjoy Fiji's cultural festivities and festivals.

Keep in mind that certain events may be restricted or interrupted due to weather conditions.

Entry Requirements, Visa Information, and Travel Documents:

Visa Requirements:

Visitors from most countries, including the United States, Canada, the United Kingdom, Australia, and New Zealand, do not need a visa for visits of up to four months.
Ensure that your passport is valid for at least six months beyond your scheduled departure date from Fiji.
Travel Documents:

A valid passport is necessary for admission into Fiji.
Check with your local embassy or consulate to determine unique admission restrictions depending on your nationality.
Arrival and Departure:

International planes arrive at Nadi International Airport (NAN) on Viti Levu, Fiji's major island.
Departure tax is normally included in the cost, but double-check with your airline.

Suggestions for Booking Flights, Accommodations, and Transportation Options inside Fiji:

Flights:

Nadi International Airport is the key gateway, providing direct flights from major cities worldwide.

Consider booking your flights early in advance to receive the cheapest pricing.

Compare costs from multiple airlines and employ flight search engines or travel websites to locate competitive offers.

Accommodations:

Fiji provides a choice of housing alternatives, including luxury resorts, hotels, budget-friendly guesthouses, and vacation rentals.

Research various places and islands to locate lodgings that fit your interests and budget.

Utilize internet travel companies, hotel booking websites, or contact local travel agents to locate the greatest rates and packages.

Transportation:

Within Fiji, domestic flights, ferry services, and boat transfers are available to travel between islands.

For island hopping, consider arranging packages or day trips that include transportation.

Taxis rented automobiles, and public buses are choices for moving about on the major islands.

Remember to verify travel advisories and any COVID-19-related recommendations or limitations before your journey, as they may affect entrance procedures, visa information, and travel arrangements.

Chapter 3

Top Destinations

Highlighting Popular Destinations in Fiji:

Nadi:

Located on the western side of Viti Levu, Nadi is Fiji's principal transportation center.
The city provides a combination of traditional Fijian culture and contemporary conveniences.
Visit the Sri Siva Subramaniya Swami Temple, the biggest Hindu temple in the southern hemisphere.
Explore the Garden of the Sleeping Giant, famed for its magnificent orchids and lush environs.
Take a plunge in the Sabeto Hot Springs and Mud Pool for a revitalizing experience.
Nadi is also the entrance to the gorgeous Mamanuca and Yasawa Islands, offering easy access to island resorts and activities.
Suva:

Suva, the capital city of Fiji, is situated on the southeastern coast of Viti Levu.

Immerse yourself in the unique cultural and historical history of Fiji.

Visit the Fiji Museum to learn about the country's history, art, and cultural treasures.

Explore the Colo-I-Suva Forest Park, a verdant rainforest with hiking paths, bathing areas, and birding.

Shop for local crafts, fresh fruit, and souvenirs at the Suva Municipal Market.

Experience the lively nightlife, with an assortment of restaurants, pubs, and clubs.

Mamanuca Islands:

The Mamanuca Islands are a popular series of islands situated off the west coast of Viti Levu.

Known for its gorgeous white-sand beaches, crystal-clear seas, and rich marine life.

Enjoy snorkeling, scuba diving, and swimming in the colorful coral reefs.

Try water activities like jet skiing, kayaking, and paddleboarding.

Relax on picture-perfect beaches or take a boat to visit numerous islands.

Castaway Island, Malolo Island, and Mana Island are among the popular sites in the Mamanuca group.

Yasawa Islands:

Located north of the Mamanuca Islands, the Yasawa Islands provide a more distant and unspoiled experience.

These islands are recognized for their spectacular vistas, quiet beaches, and colorful marine life.

Visit the Sawa-i-Lau Caves, where you may swim in subterranean tunnels filled with crystal-clear water.

Experience traditional Fijian village life and engage in cultural events and rituals.

Enjoy hiking and trekking options, discovering verdant slopes and scenic overlooks.

Yasawa Island, Waya Island, and Nanuya Levu (commonly known as Turtle Island) are famous sites in the Yasawa group.

Recommendations for Scenic Spots, Cultural Sites, and Recreational Opportunities:

Sigatoka Sand Dunes National Park: Explore Fiji's first national park, noted for its sweeping dunes, ancient monuments, and coastline vistas.

Navala community: Visit this traditional Fijian community in the highlands of Viti Levu, famed for its thatched bure homes and preserved cultural history.

Taveuni Island: Known as the "Garden Island" of Fiji, Taveuni features spectacular waterfalls, hiking paths, and the Bouma National Heritage Park.

Beqa Island: Experience traditional Fijian firewalking rites on this island, noted for its rich cultural traditions.

Bouma National Park: Located on the island of Taveuni, this park provides beautiful rainforests, waterfalls, and chances for birding and trekking.

Savusavu: A lovely village on Vanua Levu, noted for its hot springs, colorful marketplaces, and the Cousteau Resort for diving aficionados.

Chapter 4

Exploring Fijian Culture

Immersion in Fijian Traditions, Customs, and Etiquette:

Fiji is recognized for its rich cultural past, and immersing oneself in Fijian traditions, customs, and etiquette is a terrific way to experience the real spirit of the nation. Here is a full overview of Fijian culture:

Social Customs and Etiquette:

Respect for elders: Fijian culture puts significant value on giving respect to elderly folks. It is traditional to greet seniors first and address them with suitable titles such as "Marama" for women and "Turaga" for males.

Traditional greetings: The Fijian style of greeting is by saying "Bula" (pronounced boo-lah), which means "hello" or "welcome." Responding with "Bula" is typical.

Accepting Kava: Kava is a traditional Fijian drink derived from the root of the kava plant. When presenting kava at a ceremony, it is acceptable to take it with both hands and swallow it in one gulp as a symbol of respect.
Village Life and Customs:

Fijian communities preserve a strong feeling of community and traditional rituals. Visitors are invited to experience village life, but it is necessary to respect local customs and traditions. Sevusevu: When visiting a Fijian village, it is usual to deliver a sevusevu, which is a gift of kava roots, to the local chief as a show of respect and thanks.
Dress code: Modest clothes is encouraged while visiting communities. It is advisable to wear modest clothes that cover shoulders and knees as a symbol of respect.
Fijian Arts, Crafts, Music, and Dance:

Handicrafts: Fijian arts and crafts demonstrate the expertise and ingenuity of the native artists. You may discover elaborate woodcarvings, woven mats, baskets, ceramics, and traditional Fijian weaponry such as the "tanoa" (kava bowl) and "tabua" (whale's tooth).

Music: Fijian music is distinguished by heartfelt melodies, rhythmic rhythms, and lovely harmonies. Traditional Fijian music frequently contains instruments like the guitar, ukulele, lali (wooden drum), and vakalutuvi (bamboo pipes).

Dance: Fijian dance is vigorous, expressive, and strongly steeped in cultural traditions. The "meke" is a traditional dance style that incorporates narrative, rhythmic motions, and chanting. Various meke performances represent parts of Fijian history, folklore, and everyday life.

Celebrations & Festivals:

Fijians celebrate a multitude of festivals and events throughout the year. The most major festival is the Bula Festival, held yearly in Nadi, which exhibits Fijian culture via dance, music, cuisine, and traditional rites.

The Hibiscus Festival is another popular festival that incorporates beauty pageants, parades, cultural performances, and entertainment.

Cultural Sites & Museums:

Fiji Museum: Located in Suva, the Fiji Museum has a vast collection of antiques, traditional Fijian weapons, historical exhibitions, and cultural displays that give insights into Fiji's legacy.

Thurston Gardens: Adjacent to the Fiji Museum, Thurston Gardens is a beautifully designed park with walking routes, picnic spots, and historical monuments. It is a calm oasis in the center of Suva.

By immersing yourself in Fijian traditions, customs, arts, crafts, music, and dance, you will get a greater understanding of the diverse cultural tapestry of Fiji.

Chapter 5

Outdoor Adventures and Activities

Overview of Water-Based Activities:

Fiji provides a wealth of water-based activities that enable tourists to explore its beautiful marine habitats and partake in exhilarating experiences. Here is a detailed summary of popular water-based activities in Fiji:

Snorkeling and Scuba Diving:

Fiji is recognized for its great snorkeling and scuba diving possibilities. The crystal-clear seas showcase vivid coral reefs, filled with colorful fish, sea turtles, rays, and other marine life.
Some of the greatest diving destinations are the Great Astrolabe Reef in Kadavu, the Somosomo Strait in Taveuni, and the Beqa Lagoon near Pacific Harbour.
Numerous dive companies and resorts provide diving classes, guided dives, and live-aboard

experiences for divers of various levels of expertise.

Surfing:

Fiji is a surfer's paradise, drawing wave aficionados from across the globe. The islands are famous for their world-class breakers, delivering exhilarating experiences for surfers of all ability levels.

The globally recognized surf destination Cloudbreak, situated near Tavarua Island, delivers huge waves for expert surfers.

Other renowned surf breaks include Restaurants, Frigates, and Wilkes Pass in the Mamanuca Islands, as well as Desperations near the Coral Coast.

Jet Skiing, Kayaking, and Paddleboarding:

Fiji's quiet lagoons and blue seas give the ideal backdrop for jet skiing, kayaking, and paddleboarding.

Rent a jet ski or kayak to explore secret coves, uncover hidden beaches, or just enjoy the calm of the surrounding environment.

Paddleboarding is a popular pastime in Fiji, enabling you to glide through the beautiful seas while enjoying stunning coastline vistas.

Opportunities for Island Hopping, Boat Tours, and Yacht Charters:

Fiji's archipelago is formed of hundreds of islands, each with its particular beauty and attractions. Here are some possibilities for island hopping, boat excursions, and yacht rentals to make the most of your Fiji experience:

Island Hopping:

Fiji's island hopping trips enable you to tour various islands, each providing diverse landscapes, cultures, and activities.

The Mamanuca Islands and Yasawa Islands are popular island groupings, readily accessible from Nadi, and provide a choice of lodgings, activities, and gorgeous beaches.

Explore distant and unspoiled islands, explore traditional Fijian communities, and enjoy water sports and seaside leisure.

Boat Tours:

Joining a boat trip is a wonderful opportunity to see Fiji's gorgeous coasts, marine life, and hidden jewels.
Choose from a choice of boat experiences, including snorkeling excursions, sunset cruises, dolphin-watching outings, and visits to deserted islands.
Some visits include traditional Fijian rituals, cultural performances, and opportunities to connect with local people.
Yacht Charters:

For a more intimate and customized experience, consider chartering a boat in Fiji.
Yacht charters allow the flexibility to explore the islands at your speed, visit private anchorages, and find secret coves and exquisite beaches.
Charter businesses provide crewed yachts or bareboat charters, depending on your preferences and degree of sailing expertise.
Introduction to Land-Based Activities:

Fiji's beautiful vistas and lush interior provide several land-based activities for nature lovers and adventure seekers. Here are some prominent land-based activities to enjoy in Fiji:

Hiking & Trekking: Fiji provides various gorgeous hiking paths that bring you through magnificent jungles, attractive valleys, and spectacular mountains.
The Colo-I-Suva Forest Park in Suva provides well-marked paths, waterfalls, and a chance to view unusual bird species.

On the island of Taveuni, experience the Lavena Coastal Walk, a magnificent journey that takes you through coastal woods, waterfalls, and pristine beaches.
The Koroyanitu National Heritage Park in the highlands of Viti Levu provides varied routes with panoramic views, unique vegetation, and cultural sites.
Zip-lining and Canopy Tours:

Experience an adrenaline rush by flying over the trees on exhilarating zip-line experiences.

Zip-lining experiences may be available in sites such as Pacific Harbour and Taveuni, affording spectacular views of the surrounding surroundings.

Canopy excursions give you a chance to experience Fiji's gorgeous rainforests from lofty walkways and suspension bridges.

Exploring National Parks:

Fiji is home to various national parks and protected areas that exhibit the country's unique ecosystems and natural features.

The Sigatoka Sand Dunes National Park on Viti Levu contains unusual sand dunes, archaeological sites, and magnificent views of the shoreline.

Bouma National Heritage Park on Taveuni Island includes hiking routes leading to magnificent waterfalls, natural pools, and uncommon bird species.

The Nausori Highlands in the interior of Viti Levu give chances for off-road adventures, picturesque excursions, and visits to traditional Fijian communities.

Cultural Experiences:

Immerse yourself in Fijian culture by visiting local villages, partaking in traditional festivities, and mingling with the warm and hospitable Fijian people.

Join a village tour where you may learn about ancient practices, watch traditional dances and music performances, and even take part in a kava ceremony.

Visit the Arts Village at Pacific Harbour, where you can observe cultural displays, discover traditional Fijian arts and crafts, and taste real Fijian food.

Wildlife Encounters:

Fiji is home to a diversity of distinct flora and animals. Explore the Kula Eco Park in Sigatoka, which displays Fiji's biodiversity, including local birds, reptiles, and plant species.

The Kioa Island Turtle Sanctuary gives the chance to learn about sea turtle conservation initiatives and even assist in turtle releases.

Fiji's land-based activities provide a great selection of adventures, cultural experiences, and opportunities to interact with the natural beauty and traditions of the islands. From trekking through beautiful woods to immersing yourself in Fijian culture, there's plenty for everyone to enjoy on land in Fiji.

Chapter 6

Practical Tips and Safety

Health and Safety Precautions:

Stay hydrated by consuming bottled water or purified water.

Apply sunscreen frequently, since the sun in Fiji may be fierce.

Use insect repellent to guard against mosquitoes and other insects.

Follow basic hygiene habits, such as washing hands with soap and water or using hand sanitizers.

Seek medical advice before coming to Fiji about essential vaccines or prescriptions.

Currency Exchange, Communication, and Internet Access:

The official currency of Fiji is the Fijian Dollar (FJD). It is advised to exchange currency in banks, exchange offices, or authorized currency exchange booths.

Credit cards are generally accepted at hotels, resorts, and bigger enterprises. However, it is always advisable to have some cash for tiny enterprises or distant regions.

English is widely spoken in Fiji, making communication reasonably simple. Fijian and Hindi are also frequently spoken.

International roaming is accessible for most mobile networks, however, it's wise to verify with your service provider for coverage and pricing. Buying a local SIM card is an alternative for cheaper local calls and data.

Internet connectivity is provided at most hotels, resorts, and cafés. However, in more isolated regions, the connection may be restricted or slower.

Local Laws and Customs Regulations:

Respect local customs and traditions, including proper clothing rules while visiting communities, religious sites, or participating in festivities.

It is illegal to possess or use narcotics in Fiji, and penalties are harsh.

Public shows of love should be avoided, particularly in rural places, since it may be considered rude.

Same-sex partnerships are legal in Fiji, however public shows of love may be frowned upon in some areas.

It is banned to take coral or shells from the water or participate in actions that affect marine life or coral reefs.

Emergency Services and Safety:

In case of emergency, contact 911 for police, fire, or medical help. Alternatively, you may phone the National Emergency Number at 112.

Fiji has well-equipped hospitals and medical facilities in major towns and cities. It is recommended to get travel insurance that covers medical situations.

It is advisable to be careful with your stuff and utilize hotel safes or secure storage facilities for costly goods.

When swimming or engaging in water sports, always observe safety rules and be aware of current conditions and possible risks.

Transportation and Road Safety:

If hiring a vehicle, check you have a valid driver's license and educate yourself about local traffic rules and road conditions.

Public transit choices include buses and taxis. Taxis are easily accessible in metropolitan locations, although it's recommended to negotiate the fee before the ride.

Be careful while crossing roadways, since cars may not always comply with pedestrian right-of-way restrictions.

Natural Hazards:

Fiji is prone to cyclones and tropical storms, particularly during the cyclone season from November to April. Stay current with local weather predictions and follow directions from authorities in case of severe weather alerts.

Pay attention to safety requirements and caution while engaging in water sports such as snorkeling, diving, or boating. Always prioritize your safety and follow advice from qualified guides or operators.

By following these travel recommendations, you may assure a safe and happy time in Fiji. Remember to be respectful of the local culture, be educated about current situations, and take essential care to ensure your health and well-being throughout your visit.

Chapter 7

Introduction to Fijian cuisine

Fijian cuisine is a delicious combination of tastes inspired by the islands' rich cultural background, with a blend of indigenous Fijian, Indian, Chinese, and European culinary traditions. Located in the South Pacific, the archipelago of Fiji provides a feast of tropical fruits, fresh fish, and a lively palette of spices that characterize its distinct culinary identity. The cuisine of Fiji is profoundly entrenched in culture, community, and the plentiful resources of the surrounding ocean and lush land.

Traditional Dishes and Local Delicacies:

Kokoda: Kokoda is Fiji's variation on ceviche, prepared with fresh raw fish marinated in coconut milk, lime or lemon juice, onions, chiles, and other herbs. This cool meal is a classic and a must-try for seafood fans.

Lovo: Lovo is a traditional Fijian feast baked in an underground oven. It generally comprises marinated meat, such as chicken, pig, or fish, wrapped in banana leaves, and grilled over hot rocks. The slow-cooking procedure provides a smokey taste, resulting in soft and luscious meats.

Rourou: Rourou is a Fijian delicacy made from taro leaves boiled in coconut milk. The leaves are frequently blanched, coarsely minced, and combined with onions, garlic, and seasonings. Rourou is a typical complement to many Fijian dishes, offering a deep and earthy taste.

Duruka: Duruka, also known as Fijian wild asparagus, is a seasonal delicacy in Fiji. These long, thin shoots are gathered from the forest and are commonly stir-fried with onions, garlic, and seasonings. Duruka boasts a distinct flavor and texture that is much sought after by residents and tourists alike.

Palusami: Palusami is a traditional Fijian cuisine made from taro leaves packed with a combination of coconut cream, onions, garlic, and occasionally meat or fish. The packages are then wrapped in banana leaves and baked or steamed until cooked. Palusami has a rich, creamy flavor and is commonly served as a side dish.

Fiji-style Curry: The Indian influence on Fijian food is obvious in the range of curries offered. Fiji-style curries often use a variety of spices, including cumin, coriander, turmeric, and chile, cooked with meat, fish, or vegetables. These flavorful curries are generally complemented with flatbread or rice.

Cassava Cake: Cassava cake is a famous Fijian treat prepared with grated cassava, coconut milk, sugar, and spices. It is cooked till brown and has a sticky, sweet texture that is both soothing and tasty.

Popular Luxury Restaurants to Try Out:

Ivi Restaurant - Located in the center of Denarau Island, Ivi Restaurant provides an elegant dining experience with an emphasis on modern Fijian cuisine. The cuisine features locally sourced foods served with a contemporary touch, backed by a comprehensive wine selection.

Cloud 9 - For a unique eating experience, explore Cloud 9, a floating platform set in the turquoise seas of the Mamanuca Islands. This modern establishment provides wood-fired pizzas, fresh seafood, and a selection of beverages, all while enjoying panoramic views of the surrounding paradise.

Flying Fish Fiji - Situated in the Sheraton Fiji Resort, Flying Fish Fiji features a sophisticated cuisine combining Pacific-inspired dishes with a touch of cosmopolitan flare. The restaurant prides itself on employing the best local ingredients to produce inventive and aesthetically attractive culinary dishes.

Ports O' Call - Nestled inside the Denarau Yacht Club, Ports O' Call is a famous luxury restaurant that provides a fantastic dining experience. With spectacular views of the waterfront, the restaurant specializes in seafood and international cuisine. The menu provides an astonishing assortment of meals produced with the freshest locally sourced ingredients, including luscious lobster, soft fish fillets, and flavorsome Pacific-inspired delights.

Bure Restaurant - Situated inside the exclusive Namale Resort & Spa, Bure Restaurant is an exceptional dining place that symbolizes luxury. Overlooking the tranquil Koro Sea, Bure Restaurant provides a combination of world and Fijian tastes. The menu shows a broad choice of gourmet meals produced from organic ingredients, including fresh seafood, premium meats, and seasonal fruit.

Lali SandBar - Located on the scenic Malolo Island, Lali SandBar is an elegant restaurant and bar that gives an exceptional dining experience.

Surrounded by crystal-clear seas and immaculate beaches, visitors may indulge in a choice of gourmet meals while enjoying the gorgeous ocean views. The menu features a combination of Fijian and world cuisine, offering creative tastes and beautifully created meals.

Navo Restaurant - Situated inside the magnificent InterContinental Fiji Golf Resort & Spa, Navo Restaurant provides an exquisite and refined dining experience. With an emphasis on displaying the freshest local products, the restaurant delivers a sophisticated cuisine that honors Fijian tastes. Guests may eat wonderful cuisine while viewing the gorgeous Natadola Bay.

These premium restaurants in Fiji feature not only outstanding food but also breathtaking surroundings and superb service. Whether you're seeking traditional Fijian delicacies or cosmopolitan tastes with a Pacific touch, these places provide a choice of gastronomic pleasures for discriminating palates.

Remember to book appointments in advance, since these famous eateries tend to have high demand, particularly during busy tourist seasons. Enjoy the tastes of Fiji as you go on a gastronomic adventure across its rich and varied culinary environment.

Chapter 8

Sustainability and Responsible Tourism

Insight into Fiji's Environmental Conservation Efforts:

Fiji is recognized for its magnificent natural beauty, clean beaches, bright coral reefs, and lush jungles. Recognizing the necessity of conserving these distinct ecosystems, Fiji has made major efforts toward environmental conservation and sustainability. Here are some major programs and organizations contributing to Fiji's conservation efforts:

Fiji's Protected Areas: Fiji has built a network of protected areas, including maritime parks, nature reserves, and animal sanctuaries. These zones strive to conserve fragile ecosystems, endangered animals, and traditional cultural places. Examples include the Yasawa Islands Marine Protected Area and the Bouma National Heritage Park on Taveuni Island.

Coral Reef Conservation: Fiji is part of the Coral Triangle, a region noted for its extraordinary marine biodiversity. Conservation groups, such as the Wildlife Conservation Society of Fiji and the Fiji Locally Managed Marine Area (FLMMA) network, work diligently to safeguard Fiji's coral reefs via research, monitoring, and community participation.

Reforestation & Forest Conservation: Fiji has developed reforestation efforts to counteract deforestation and maintain its important forests. The Fiji Forests and Protected Areas Committee, together with groups like NatureFiji-MareqetiViti and the World Wildlife Fund (WWF), concentrates on encouraging sustainable forestry practices and creating awareness about the value of forests.

Sustainable Fisheries: The Fiji government, in partnership with organizations like the Fiji Fisheries Department and the Fiji Locally Managed Marine Area (FLMMA) network, supports sustainable fishing techniques. Initiatives include community-based fisheries management, creating marine protected zones, and enforcing legislation to avoid overfishing.

Tips for Practicing Responsible Tourism:

Respect the Environment: When visiting Fiji, be conscious of the endangered ecosystems. Avoid harming coral reefs, do not litter, and use established trails when visiting woods and natural areas. Practice Leave No Trace principles and take only memories, leaving behind just footprints.

Support Sustainable Accommodation: Choose lodgings that have incorporated eco-friendly measures such as energy conservation, trash management, and water-saving programs. Look for eco-certifications like EarthCheck or Rainforest Alliance certification.

Conserve Water and Energy: Be careful of water and energy use throughout your stay. Take shorter showers, reuse towels, switch off lights and air conditioning when not in use, and disconnect gadgets when not required.

Minimize Single-Use Plastics: Fiji has taken steps to eliminate single-use plastics, and you can participate by bringing reusable water bottles, bags, and straws. Refill your water bottle from trusted sources or seek hotels that have filtered water stations.

Support Local Conservation Initiatives: Research and support local conservation groups and initiatives in Fiji. Some organizations provide volunteer opportunities that enable you to actively contribute to conservation efforts.

Recommendations for Supporting Local Communities and Engaging in Cultural Exchanges:

Support Local Businesses: Choose locally owned motels, eateries, and tour operators. This helps to direct tourist earnings to local communities, supporting economic development and empowerment.

Participate in Cultural Experiences: Engage in cultural exchanges by engaging in traditional rituals, visiting local communities, and supporting indigenous crafts and arts. Respect local customs and traditions, obtain permission before taking images, and be open to learning about Fijian culture.

Learn Some Fijian Phrases: Learning a few simple Fijian phrases, such as welcome and thank-yous, demonstrates respect and admiration for the local language and culture. It may also help you connect with locals on a more intimate basis.

Support Community-based Tourism: Seek chances to participate in community-based tourism programs that enable you to connect with local communities and learn about their way of life. This may include homestays, cultural excursions, and village visits done in partnership with local community groups or travel providers. By engaging in these activities, you directly support the local economy and contribute to the well-being of the communities.

Respect Local Customs and Traditions: Fiji has a rich cultural background, and it's crucial to respect and appreciate local customs and traditions. Seek direction from local hosts or guides on acceptable conduct, dress modestly while visiting villages or religious places, and always ask for permission before taking pictures.

Purchase Locally manufactured items: Support local craftsmen and crafters by purchasing locally manufactured items and souvenirs. This helps to perpetuate traditional arts and crafts and gives economic possibilities for local communities. Look for handicraft markets or cooperatives where you may get original and locally manufactured things.

Participate in Volunteering or Community Service: Consider engaging in community service initiatives or volunteering opportunities that concentrate on environmental protection, education, or community development. This enables you to actively contribute to the well-being of local communities and make a positive impression during your stay.

By following this advice, you may help to the preservation of Fiji's natural environment, assist local people, and participate in important cultural exchanges. Remember, responsible tourism is about leaving a good impact and establishing a sustainable future for both the environment and the people of Fiji.